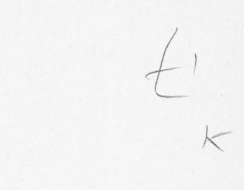

D1463865

FROM THE SONNET HISTORY OF MODERN POETRY

*From the Sonnet History of
Modern Poetry*

Poems by John Whitworth

Illustrations by Gerald Mangan

PETERLOO POETS

First published in 1999
by Peterloo Poets
2 Kelly Gardens, Calstock, Cornwall PL18 9SA, U.K.

**A catalogue record for this book is available
from the British Library**

ISBN 1-871471-79-6

Printed in Great Britain by
Latimer Trend & Company Ltd, Plymouth

I began writing these poems in 1994 and sent some to a poet friend of mine who didn't care for them much. Oh dear, I thought, and tried three on P.J. Kavanagh at *The Spectator*. He took them all, an unusually gratifying result. A couple of months later one was solicited for an American religious magazine called *First Things*, and therefore earned money *twice*. I began constructing more of these marvellously saleable commodities.

The Spectator changed editors. Frank Johnson didn't care for my poetry, indeed for any poetry at all and the magazine no longer prints it — a pity that. So I bundled up about fifteen sonnets and sent them to Peter Forbes at *Poetry Review*. He phoned after an interval to say he would like to print one in each issue for an unspecified time. Actually, he began with two, the second (Wright and Dunn) brilliantly illustrated by Gerald Mangan. 'More of these!' I cried. And we did have more.

'*From the Sonnet History* . . . ' I hope puts a stop to all that stuff about 'Why *this* poet and not *that* poet?' I've got them *all* on copious files, see.

They *are* all sonnets according to me, though you'll stretch the definition a bit for some. Two were written (guess which!) because Gerald already had drawings. The others happened the other way round. **J.W.**

To Doreen

Contents

American Pie (Cantata For Two Voices)

BASS:
I'm rough and tough. I smoke and drink and swear.
To hell with European airs and graces.
I'm wild and woolly as a grizzly bear.
I write Free Verse, untamed and in my braces.

Modernism starts here. You've got it all. He writes down what pops into his head and to hell with editing. She invents the dash as another way of PUTTING READERS IN THEIR PLACE. Absolute gifts for the Literature Industry. No-one could read the whole of *Leaves of Grass* without being paid to do so, and Emily is too agreeably off her head for there not to have been plenty of lookalikes in everything but talent — more in the US of course but there's more of everything over there.

SOPRANO:
I call on Fame —who never called on me —
I keep my Language — like my body — chaste —
I write a thousand Poems — publish three —
My Art is perfect — though my Life is waste.

DUET:
We are the People, following the sun,
We are the Gods, electric with creating,
The Brooklyn bounder and the Amherst nun,
New ways of seeing, being — punctuating —
We are the stars of hope, the stripes of sorrow.
We are America. We are Tomorrow.

Mangan 97

Performance Poet

I sing a man born in 1830 and dead
A year before the 'good and charitable Sovereign' to whom
    he wrote his
Famous Jubilee Ode. I sing a man said
To be 'the greatest bad poet of his age'— the quote is

From *Punch*, not-notably-poetic organ of the Philistines.
Many a poet (Yeats for instance) is an unconscious
    comedian,
And our man's works mature like the finest wines,
For I sing Willam McGonagall, 'Poet and Tragedian ',

Whose influence on English and Scottish poetry will never
    ever fade,
Who performed, 'in a strong voice with great enthusiasm',
    causing streets to be crowded 'from head to foot', and
    multitudes to weep all,
Who was a poor man, living for his art, a weaver by
    trade,
Like Bully Bottom, another poet of the people.

So, 'in stentorian voices as loud as we can bawl' let us
    give three hearty cheers
To one of our bardic persuasion whose works have been
    continuously in print for over A HUNDRED YEARS!

ROME
MDCCCLXXIV

The Chesterbelloc Knighterrant Versemachine

O the Chesterbelloc's out to slay his dragons —
Down the rolling English road behold him ride
Quaffing English ale in rolling English flagons
With a rolling English rosary by his side.

They're all horrid foreign dragons, often Jewish
Or American (though the Frenchies are OK),
And the virgins are delightful, never shrewish,
And the sun shines on the English every day.

And each Englishman's a dietary nutter,
Beer for breakfast and a pig out in the shed,
So he's permanently pissed and fat as butter
And he never has an illness till he's dead.

Then his English soul will roll to Paradise
Which is English too, and very, very nice.

A poet told me that nobody reads Chesterton and Belloc these days, which just shows how much HE knows. A better one said I shouldn't be attacking them like the trendy creeps, a serious charge. But I love my Chesterbelloc and this isn't an ATTACK, Good Heavens.

The Gods

The Gods made Art and Poetry and they
All died within the memory of Men.
We tried and failed to find fresh things to say,
So dug them up and buried them again.

In chiselled verses chaste as Ancient Greek
And enigmatic as the pyramids,
Myth and allusion played at hide-and-seek,
Something about the workers and the yids,

Something about a secret that the Low
(The festering filthy and the filthy rich)
Will never understand, will never know.
Who's in, who's out, what's what and which is which,

Something about the Blood, the Mystery,
Madness and Race and Ambiguity.

This is the poem those religious Americans wanted. Yeats ought to be over on the
other page too but you can find him a page or two later sharing a less crowded spot
with Robert Graves.

War Poets

'What poems do I like? Do you mean for *fun*?'
I nod. She frowns, 'We do First World War stuff.'
'No nightingales or daffodils?'
                                        'No, none.'
The young today must take their poems tough.

Those real and relevant War Poets died —
Owen and Brooke and Rosenberg — and some
Let off the dying, got screwed up inside.
Their Muse went mad, or blind, or deaf, or dumb.

This peaceful poet's done his stint. And she,
To show me out, has dodged her English class.
She frowns again, 'I hate war poetry!
Goodbye.' Her sandals shimmer through the grass.

Where'er she walks the insistent flowers spread,
And choirs of songbirds flutter round her head.

Every word is true, even the sandals — Dr Scholl's they were. Of course it's not the fault of Owen and the rest if their stuff is smuggled into a syllabus by anti-poetry teachers (of whom there are a good number) as history or whatever, but I'm glad if it doesn't work. Bring back de la Mare. I bet she'd like him. And she'd be right.

Opium of the People

When Science knocked Religion off its perch
The poets nailed the parrot back. They tried
Pretending God had never really died.
His soul lived on, you see. A thorough search

Would find it hidden somewhere in the church.
Poetry was a beacon and a guide
To counter scientific deicide,
Not leave the poor believer in the lurch.

When Blake drew Enitharmon and Urizen
When Yeats sang gyres, when henpecked Robert Graves
Made a White Goddess out of Laura Riding,
When Eliot glumly told you Jesus Saves,
You thought a God (or Goddess) must be hiding,

But were those poets having all you guys on?

The atheistical and witty philosopher, David Hume, got stuck in an Edinburgh bog
and, being very fat, he couldn't climb out. A pious old woman gave him assistance
but only after he had recited The Lord's Prayer. She thought he couldn't, but he
could and did.

Hundred Proof Scotch

Dr Grieve is working class and lets you know it
And he's hard as Uncle Joe, and what he earns
He deserves for being Scotland's first real poet
Since Dunbar and Henryson. NOT bloody Burns!

Damn that sentimental fake, that English quisling!
Damn that fornicating tool of the Excise!
Dr Grieve's fierce Scots moustache commences bristling.
Damn the bourgeois, damn their traitrous English eyes,

Damn the ancient enemies of Hugh McDiarmid!
As the tide of good Scotch whisky laps in gallons
Round his Scots Renaissance, no-one gets a permit
As a poet if they don't compose in Lallans.

For a Makar to be truly atmospheric
Not a soul should understand him south of Berwick.

Poetic Licence and yes, I do know about MacCaig. Perhaps I should explain that
Uncle Joe was an affectionate(?) nickname for Stalin, our wartime ally. When
Bulganin and Kruschev visited Britain not long after the old swine's death, students
would sing 'Poor Old Joe' at them. MacDiarmid was an unreconstructed Stalinist,
the type was common in Scotland where political extremism is a Sunday hobby.
Nationalists in my childhood used to blow up pillar boxes with EIIR on them, first
checking the contents for postal orders, no doubt.

Strike Me Pink: a Parable for the Sixties

Paint me commitment. Paint me Bertholt Brecht,
A reputation at its apogee:
THE GREATEST WRITER OF THE CENTURY
(Grovelling adulation raged unchecked),

A PLAYWRIGHT with the courage to reject
Bourgeois conventions — like scenery,
Learning the lines and speaking properly,
His famous alienation effect —

A MORALIST who'd sell his mother's life
To keep his red nose clean with Uncle Joe,
A POET plundering poems from his wife,
His mistress, any woman apropos,
To pass off as his own, Old Bert The Knife,
The Age's Ape, the Age's Horrorshow.

Unfair. I can't read German so he might be very good indeed. Not a nice man
though, and without the genius of Kurt Weil — definitively nice — wouldn't *The
Threepenny Opera* have sunk like a stone? Like a stone, and like Auden's 'The
Ascent of F6' and most of Eliot's verse plays.

The Ulster Camel and the English Queer

This sprawling boy's big face is like the moon.
He has big, pale hands. He smokes and makes a noise,
Goes to the pictures every afternoon,
Also (he says) fucks all the other boys

Back in his curtained, smoky poet's room.
Except the broody Ulster Camel — he
Won't play the game by Wystan's rules, his doom
Is booze and women and the BBC.

Wystan becomes American and falls
In love, his lunar visage cracks and seams
Like life. His poems have us by the balls,
Their rhymes and metres jangle in our dreams.

But Louis's difficult and fails to fit,
Much like his birthplace, come to think of it.

MacSpaunday was a four man pantomime horse originally, but Time, probably
unfairly, has cut it down to two. The 'Camel' remark (very apt) is not my own but
made by one of his wives.

Roaring Forties

Who won the War? The bloody Yanks, but never
Poor bloody us, no strut, no style, no cash,
Just power-cuts, ration-books and queues forever.
But Art is free and Art should make a splash.

We want extravagance and ormolu,
Black market nylons, marzipan and waste.
Great God! We've had enough of making do,
High mindedness and horrible good taste.

We've had enough of the austerely English.
We want the vatic chant, the Celtic mist,
Poems that leave you out-of-breath and tinglish,
Poems that leave you feeling slightly pissed.

The *Zeitgeist* labours with ecstatic cries,
And Dylan Thomas squalls between her thighs.

Dylan used to drink with John Arlott (although of course he used to drink with
absolutely anybody). Is there a thesis to be written on Thomas and cricket, with
reference to Glamorgan's County Championship in 1948?

Mrs Parker and Stevie

Mrs Parker's thing was raising hell.
Out with the boys, boy, could she wise a crack!
Her other thing was Love. She always fell
For pretty jerks who couldn't love her back.

Stevie lived all her life in Palmers Green,
Much with her Lion Aunt. She was a secretary,
Who wrote three novels, seven books of poetry
And talked (this was mischief) of hoovers to the Queen

Whose medal she received for her poetry.
She speaks with the authority of sadness
Said Larkin memorably. So they both spoke,
Stevie and Mrs Parker, with sad authority.

And wit, which is important. Though Life's no joke,
Wit keeps them at bay, the wolves, the wolves of suicide
    and madness.

The Queen asked Stevie Smith where she got her ideas for poems. 'When I'm hoovering,' said Stevie. I've forgotten what the Queen (who looks like a frenetic hooverer) said next.

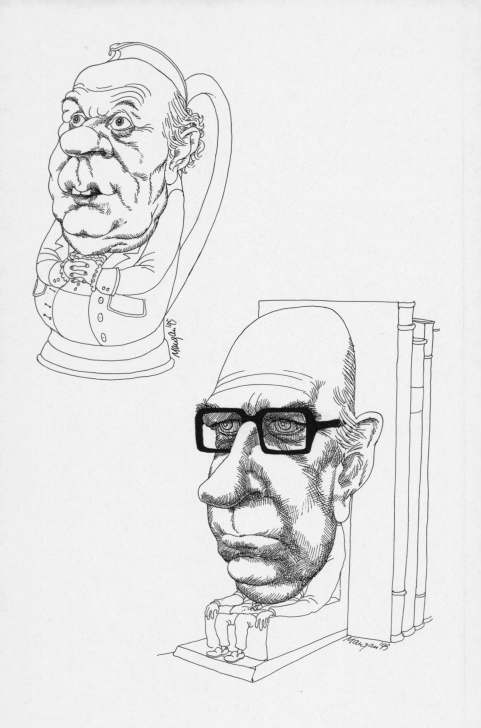

Big Phil and Uncle John

We studied hard. We tried to get to grips
With Modernism, but we couldn't hack it,
A beastly, leftist, highbrow foreign racket,
French to its garlic-sodden fingertips.

Masefield and Rupert Brooke had had their chips.
Surely the time had come for us to pack it
In, break the pipe and sell the hairy jacket?
Then we discovered Big Phil's cycle clips:

Crumpled lugubriousness in plain man's chat,
Moaning and muttering fuck from time to time,
The essential Englisheness of being odd,
Uncle John's teddy bear and scrumpy hat,

Victorian values and Victorian rhyme,
Worrying. About Sex. And Death. And God.

Betjeman's Archibald was a model for the teddy of ghastly Sebastian in *Brideshead Revisited*. Difficult to imagine Larkin with one of those, unless it was Eeyore. Or Ted Hughes (Ted's Ted)? THERE's an anthology idea!

The Wild Good Lookers

The wild good lookers: Thom in biker's leather
Has crashed his Harley on the Freeway twice.
Ted keeps on splashing out in filthy weather,
Filling his Barbour pockets with dead mice.

A Poet's life is lived along the edge
Of savage rhythms and primaeval surges.
We feel it when our neighbour trims his hedge
And won't sweep up the clippings from the verges.

To hell with smug, suburban platitudes —
We're on the move and Man, we gotta go.
What is it hunches on the gate and broods?

It seemed to be a hawk but it's a crow.
The neolithic forest sleeps beneath.
We were not born to die in Hayward's Heath.

This poem was quoted (in part) in the Peterborough column of *The Daily Telegraph*.
Poetry in the *Telegraph* — that's really refreshing the parts other bards . . .

Something

'But what happens if I get old or something?'
Asked the most famous poet on the planet
Really wanting to know. What happens if
My face collapses like a pomegranate
And nothing works to keep my pecker stiff
And Peter doesn't love me? It's a dumb thing,
A glum, thing, numb thing, if you get old or something.

'People will always like you. You're a nice person.'
A good answer, most of us would agree,
From a good shrink, the famous poet's friend.
It handed him permission to be free,
And people did always like him. If near the end
Poor Peter got shot to hell, some things do worsen
When you're old or something, for even the nicest person.

A '60s conversation recorded in *Ginsberg* by Barry Miles. I'm never sure how much
Ginsberg is sending himself up and how much he is a GENUINE American
McGonagall. A professor of course later on, but never did the weaving as far as I
know.

EXEGI MONUMENTUM LIBRO PERENNIUS

Concrete and Clay

If Edwin Morgan were to wear this sonnet
He wouldn't wear it like a bowler hat
But with a rakish twist, the auld Scots bonnet

Like _{this} . . .

    or **THIS** . . .

                                  h s
               or t   i   . . . or t
                                        h
                                        i
                                        s

                                or . . .

. . . **SPLATT!**

    AND*IAN*HAMILTON*FINLAY
    WOULD*EMPLOY*INSTEAD
    TEAK*BRASS*INLAY
    AND*FLOWER*BED

old Guillaume Apollinaire
liked to play with his french teepwreetaire

e e cummings showed wit and grace
frisking about in the lower case

and cockroach archy & mehibatel
but wotthehell wotthehell

I always thought that cummings stole the title of his autobiographical *The Enormous Room* from Auden. But since e e cummings published it in 1922, the theft must have been the other way round.

Poetry With Balls

Who is Sylvia? Which twin has the Tony?
You throw a load of mud and plenty sticks,
You read a lot of verse and most is phony,
You throw Big Daddy in the Magimix,

The worst are loaded and the best are stony,
The literary world is all a fix,
A whippet's better than a polo pony,
It's bleedin' Class. It's not. It's effin' Pricks.

Who smuggled out the map? Who bribed the garrison?
Who dropped the Muse into the acid bath?
Who wove a word-robe rich beyond comparison?
Who turned the poet to a psychopath?
Which has the Tony? Jeeze! It must be Harrison.
And who is Sylvia? Christ! It must be Plath.

'Which Twin Has the Toni?' was an advertising slogan about a shampoo or a home perm, I forget which.

Hard Ham and Old Al

O the critics are coming! Their hoofbeats are drumming.
There's blood on their saddles, they shoot for the heart.
Poets, cease from your strumming, come-uppance is coming,
They'll hang you up high or they'll blow you apart,

Yes, Old Al and Hard Ham, they just don't give a damn,
They are Marshals most partial to laying down Laws
For the badlands of po-biz. You bleed and that's showbiz,
They flay with a phrase and they gore with a clause.

With a quip to the head they can drop you stone dead,
And your couplets are clinker, your sonnets are earth,
All your prosody dust is. Their poetic justice
Has throttled your poor little Muselet at birth.

BUT . . .
    the po-prosecutors have hung up their shooters
and, gentle as Thyrsis now,
                    pen little verses now.

It is odd that the fiercest critics often write the most anodyne verse. Geoffrey
Grigson was another, and even Matthew Arnold never let half the wicked energy of
his prose spill over into poems.

The Long and the Short of It

We poets are a proud race. Day and night
When and wherever alcohol may be
Consumed without financial penalty
We meet to praise the craft. Here's tall Kit Wright

Beaming above the passion and the fight
With disconnected geniality.
His English charm is like his poetry;
Simple straightforwardness that isn't quite.

Next to him Douglas Dunn is bearded, terse,
With serious glasses hooding serious eyes.
He writes a Scottish, clotted kind of verse.
And he is very short, contrariwise.

I dedicate this picture to the Muse
Who chooses poets. Poets do not choose.

I confess I have never actually met Douglas Dunn. If there is a shorter living poet of
his eminence, then I apologise. Being photographed with Larkin does tend to shrink
you a bit. Physically I mean.

Lord of Misrule

Respectfully, Your Majesty, the time
Is ripe that you bestow a gracious gong,
On one more riddling Mendicant of Rhyme
Who'll bear the Torch of Poetry along.

Sir Stephen and Sir John who burned so bright
Are gone, and Mr Larkin CBE
Who died too soon at scarcely sixty-three
Before he could mature into a Knight.

Here's Autumn then, with April at his heart,
(The years have turned him rich and sweet like chutney),
The Doyen of Terpsichorean Art,
The People's Choice, the Laureate of Putney.

Arise Sir Gavin! Or, if you would do it
Righter than right, Ma'am, rise FIRST BARON EWART!

Alas too late. I miss Gavin at Poetry Society do's and those pyrotechnic verbal
displays will no longer be illuminating odd corners. But in Elysium he is a Baron.

Squandering Words Like a Millionaire

Jolly Jim Fenton used to take the piss
At School, while serious longhairs howled the moon.
I think we ought to honour him for this;
Verse is like sex; it often comes too soon.

Later at Oxford (well, where did you think?)
The Meadow trees were thick with bardic moonies.
'Stuff this!' cried Jolly Jim, 'I'll be a shrink
And make a living from the other loonies.'

But no! The World of Work saw Jolly Jim
Get on his unpoetic journo's bike
And find abroad. Perhaps abroad found him —
You know what these *New Statesman* chaps are like.

Now he's a poet and a millionaire
And made it out of writing verse, so there!

Millionaire seems unlikely, but it was on 'Desert Island Discs' so must be true. It's
connected with Cameron Mackintosh but, in The Arts these days, what isn't?

The Voice of the Bard

Protestant or Catholic?
I'm Jewish.
Protestant Jewish or Catholic Jewish?

I write these lines in praise of Seamus Famous
Who scooped the Nobel Prize and rightly so.
There's not a lot big Seamus doesn't know
About our Craft. An Oxford Prof, the same as

Auden and Graves, he is no ignoramus
But wears his learning lightly, with a show
Of Irish charm that's every inch the pro
And never gets reptilian or squamous.

The rest of us are tempted and we fall:
We hone the edge of literary malice;
We join the politicians' hokey-cokey.

But Seamus, in a voice as thick and smoky
As Irish Malt, rejects the poisoned chalice,
Smooth and urbane as any cardinal.

Though it was Yeats (of course it was) who dreamt of being a cardinal, Seamus
Heaney looks MUCH more like one.

The Irish Question

What is it? Something in the Irish air?
The rain, the treacly stout, the politics —
The bloodymindedness that does not care
For English Arts of Compromise and Fix

And Smooth-tongued Lying too. But no, we will
Not talk of that. Let's talk of books and such.
An Englishman takes Culture like a pill —
Good medicine but doesn't like it much.

Poets are criminals, or drunk, or loony
Or (which is much the same) apart and holy.
An Irish poet might be you, or you . . .

Muldoon, McGuckian, Mahon, Montague,
Carson, Simmons, Boland, Longley, Foley,
Kinsella, Farrell, Durcan, Paulin, Mooney . . .

. . . Daugherty, Sweeney, Byrom, Dallat, Dawe
And (bloody English rhyme) a hundred more.

One would like to believe it was an Irish plot or a publishers' plot or something.
But there just seem to be a lot of Irish poets about the place. Most unfair.

'Perra' = two, as, 'Erra perra toon coonseloors!' (Behold two Scottish intellectuals!)
Roger Garfitt in *Poetry Review* thinks Caribbean dialect is OK but Scots isn't — a
position difficult to sustain, I would have thought. I've checked my dialect with
Gerald and Oor Wullie in *The Sunday Post* but I doubt it passes muster with the
great Tom Leonard. Free Scotland should give him some kind of tartan gong — if
they (or he come to that) believe in such things.

Floor o Scoatlinn

Perra poyetz doon the Doric fer a bevvy.
Thuz Tom Leonard watchin Warl Cup — Scoatlinn playz
So pathetic he's fair greetin in his heavy —
Thuz Liz Lochead oan aboot her hoalidayz

Doon in Eejip. 'Crivvens, Tom. There's this terrific
Perra statcha's feet aw hackt affa the kneez.
An writ roond aboot, in auld-style hyra-gliffick:
AW YIZ PEZZINTS GRUVL! AH AM THE BIG CHEEZ

AN MA TEMPER IZZ THAT BAD IZZ DIE-A-BOLLICKLE!
LOOK OAN MA WURKZ, YI BASTUDZ, AN DESPAIR!
Dizzit no make yi ponder? Dead symbolickle —
Jist two big feet ter say LIFE IZNY FAIR.'

Answerz Tom, 'A bitter cup — ah've drunk ma fill.
MAROCKA THREE, AND SCOATLINN BLUDDY NIL.'

A Hard Raine's Gonna Fall

'Long Tom' Eliot was Pope and ruled at Faber.
He dispensed poetic justice like Lord Reith.
And a bard was counted worthy of his labour
When the Mitre passed to 'Silver-tongue' Monteith.

But the brazen Age of Market Forces came and
How we trembled in the bistros and the bars
As the Holy Chair was given to the flame and
A Barbarian Vandal shuttled in from Mars.

For this alien, as dandy as Beau Brummell,
Sold a book of filthy poetry for gain
And composed a sort of sonnet to his bumhole —
Must we kneel and kiss the ring of 'Acid' Raine?

No! New springs of Helicon shall drench Queen Square
And after Raine a Reid shall flourish there.

Charles Monteith was the editor (later Chairman of ff)who kept soliciting Larkin
for poems — like a priest asking why there aren't more little ones — the poet
complained testily, though I can't locate the remark in the *Life* or the *Letters*. I
should point out that the book of filthy poetry was not Craig Raine's. It was *The
Faber Book of Blue Verse*, edited by me — after the poisoned chalice had been
rejected by a number of others — but Raine's brainchild.

Dead Sheep

There's some lost souls out there think Art is deep,
Inspiring and uplifting, suchlike guff.
It's a Post-Modern world and you want stuff
Like that! I swear it makes a critic weep.

So wise up, wankers: ART IS ABOUT DEAD SHEEP.
That Timeless Beauty junk, it's not enough.
The cutting edge today is rough and tough
And makes your boring, bourgeois values creep.

This Peter Reading is the man to read.
He'll cause your sensibilities to bleed,
Decapitated, disembowelled, throttled,

Or celebrate more contemplative deaths
By derv, by brasso, lighter fuel or meths,
Though for himself he takes it Chateau bottled.

I went to a Reading by Reading at the old Poetry Society building and finished up
drinking someone else's wine in the next door garden with Eddie Linden. I'm sorry
I missed the poems but it seemed appropriate.

Strugnell's Incredible Lightness of Being

I am a Modern Poet. People say
It's difficult to understand my stuff.
I tell them they're not up-to-date enough.
That's how it is with Poetry today.

I am a Modern Poet. And a bloke.
Most of us are. I think while Man creates
Woman inspires and appreciates.
Frankly, most Women's poems are a joke:

Their sonnets scan. Their rondels rhyme. And worse.
Their volumes SELL! Of course they cannot hope
To pass as poets in the Modern manner.
I scorn to live next door to Sophie Hannah.

No cocoa will I take with Wendy Cope.
Girls can't write Poetry.
                          They write Light Verse.

I feel I've hit on something here. Fewer women do write the pompous, portentous
stuff like . . . oh you know. Of course they bang on rather about other things.

To Iceland for Frozen Vegeburgers

See Glyn and Simon, big Post-Modern guns,
Where geysers spout, where mountains have a mist on,
Where phone books bulge with Magnus Magnussons!
Which poet's Louis then, and which is Wystan?

Glyn's verses splutter on the tongue like sherbet,
Simon's more ruminative-like, much more chewy.
If Glynn's John Donne, Simon must be George Herbert.
But which is Wystan then, and which is Louis?

Which grew a poet's beard, which rode, I pray you,
A poet's horse and fell off on his arse?
Ah which is Louis, which is Wystan, say you,
As history repeats itself as farce?

After the Moderns, the post Moderns came
And they are different. They are not the same.

Glyn Maxwell and Simon Armitage visited Iceland just as Auden and MacNiece had
done before them. A publisher's duff idea, I think, and I suppose I would have done
it too if money had been offered. Nevertheless . . .